LAUGH-OUT-LOUD JOKES

LAUGH-OUT-LOUD SCIENCE JOKES

BY LEONA FOWLER

WINDMILL BOOKS

Published in 2026 by Windmill Books, an Imprint of Rosen Publishing
2544 Clinton St., Buffalo, NY 14224

Copyright © 2026 by The Rosen Publishing Group, Inc.

All rights reserved. No part of this book may be reproduced in any form without permission in writing from the publisher, except by a reviewer.

First Edition

Editor: Caitie McAneney
Book Design: Claire Zimmermann

Photo Credits: Cover, p.1 (child laughing) Prostock-studio/Shutterstock.com; series art (paper texture) OanaGherghe2/Shutterstock.com; series art (illustrations throughout) Look_Studio/Shutterstock.com; series art (illustrations) pp. 10, 12, 14, 20 Nadzin/Shutterstock.com; p. 5 (left) Raul Mellado Ortiz/Shutterstock.com, (right) beeboys/Shutterstock.com; p. 7 (right) Sumala Chidchoi/Shutterstock.com, (left) Pyty/Shutterstock.com; p. 9 Mike Laptev/Shutterstock.com; p. 11 Max kegfire/Shutterstock.com; p. 13 WESTOCK PRODUCTIONS/Shutterstock.com; p. 15 John Arehart/Shutterstock.com; p. 17 Illonajalll/Shutterstock.com; p. 19 sezer66/Shutterstock.com; p. 21 Krakenimages.com/Shutterstock.com.

Some of the images in this book illustrate individuals who are models. The depictions do not imply actual situations or events.

Library of Congress Cataloging-in-Publication Data

Names: Fowler, Leona author
Title: Laugh-out-loud science jokes / Leona Fowler.
Description: Buffalo, NY : Windmill Books, 2026. | Series: Laugh-out-loud jokes | Includes index. | Audience term: Children
Identifiers: LCCN 2025009597 (print) | LCCN 2025009598 (ebook) | ISBN 9781538399231 (library binding) | ISBN 9781538399224 (paperback) | ISBN 9781538399248 (ebook)
Subjects: LCSH: Science–Juvenile humor | Wit and humor, Juvenile | LCGFT: Humor
Classification: LCC PN6231.S4 F69 2026 (print) | LCC PN6231.S4 (ebook)
LC record available at https://lccn.loc.gov/2025009597
LC ebook record available at https://lccn.loc.gov/2025009598

Manufactured in the United States of America

CPSIA Compliance Information: Batch #CSWM26. For further information, contact Rosen Publishing at 1-800-237-9932

CONTENTS

Laughs in the Lab 4
Chemistry Comedy 6
Silly Cells 8
Atom Antics. 10
Super Space Jokes. 12
Science Rocks. 14
Wacky Weather 16
Life Cycles 18
Brainy Bits 20
Glossary 22
For More Information 23
Index 24

Words in the glossary appear in **bold** the first time they are used in the text.

LAUGHS IN THE LAB

Why did the cell cross the microscope?
TO GET TO THE OTHER SLIDE.

How do scientists get fresh breath?
EXPERI-MINTS.

Why couldn't the biologist find the virus on his microscope?
IT FLU AWAY!

How did the trendsetter scientist burn her hand?
SHE TOUCHED THE BEAKER BEFORE IT WAS COOL.

FUN FACT!
Most cells are so small you need a tool called a microscope to make them look bigger.

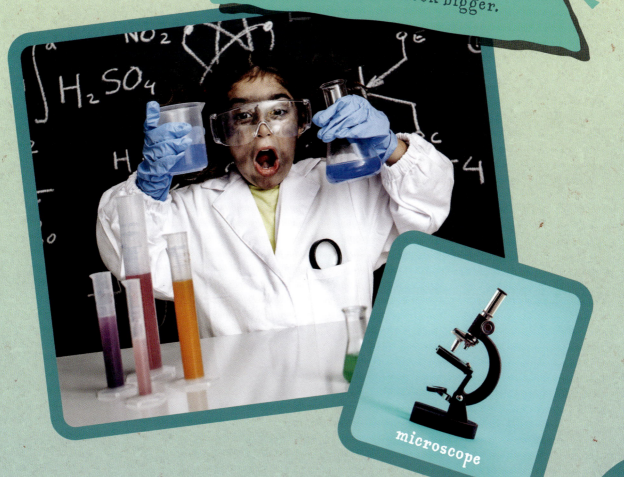

microscope

5

CHEMISTRY COMEDY

Why are chemists good at fixing problems?
THEY HAVE ALL THE SOLUTIONS.

Where do chemists eat lunch?
AT THE PERIODIC TABLE.

How often should you tell chemistry jokes?
ONLY PERIODICALLY.

Why did the scientists break up with one another?
THERE WAS NO CHEMISTRY.

FUN FACT!

The periodic table orders elements, which are the building blocks of everything that exists.

PERIODIC TABLE

SILLY CELLS

What instrument do biologists like best?
A CELL-O.

What did one strand of DNA say to the other?
"NICE GENES!"

How do biologists call one another?
ON THEIR CELL PHONES.

What do you call a picture of a bacteria?
A CELL-FIE.

FUN FACT!

DNA holds all the information about your genes. It's like a blueprint for the body! Every one of your cells has DNA in it.

ATOM ANTICS

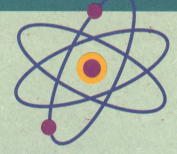

Why are protons optimists?
THEY ARE ALWAYS POSITIVE.

Why can't you trust atoms?
THEY MAKE UP EVERYTHING.

Why aren't electrons fun to hang out with?
THEY'RE ALWAYS SO NEGATIVE.

What did the physicist say when he wanted to fight?
"LET ME ATOM!"

10

FUN FACT!

Atoms are the basic units of all matter. They have parts with a positive charge, called protons, and parts with a negative charge, called electrons.

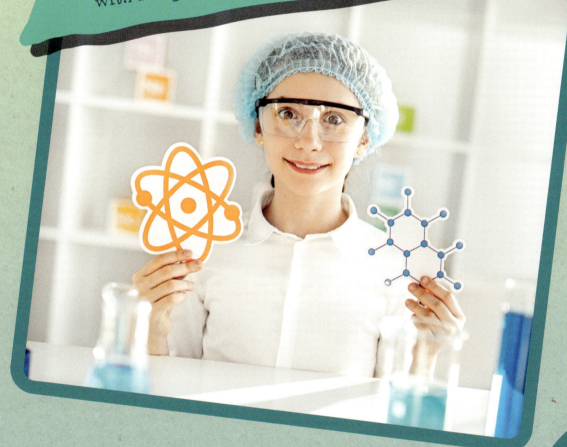

11

SUPER SPACE JOKES

What happens if you read a book on zero gravity?
YOU CAN'T PUT IT DOWN!

What's the first step in throwing a space party?
YOU PLANET.

What is a planet's favorite kind of music?
NEPTUNES.

Why is Saturn always in style?
IT WEARS SO MANY RINGS!

FUN FACT!

Astronauts use "zero gravity" to describe feeling weightless, or floating, in space—where there is less gravity than on Earth.

SCIENCE ROCKS

What did the **tectonic plate** say when it bumped its neighbor?
"SORRY, MY FAULT!"

Why are **sedimentary rocks** so cheap?
THEY'RE ALWAYS ON SHALE.

What music do geologists like?
ROCK.

What do you call a fake stone in Ireland?
A SHAM-ROCK.

FUN FACT!

Geology is the study of the things that make up the earth, such as soil, rocks, and minerals.

WACKY WEATHER

What did the tree say to the lightning?
"YOU'RE SHOCKING!"

What kind of clothing do storm clouds have?
THUNDERWEAR.

Guess what happened when I tried to catch fog.
I MIST!

What happens when it rains cats and dogs?
YOU MIGHT STEP IN A POODLE!

FUN FACT!

Lightning is a huge spark of electricity. Earth sees almost 100 lightning bolts every second.

LIFE CYCLES

You know the funny thing about butterflies? THEY'RE NOT WHAT THEY USED TO BE!

Why didn't the tadpole smile? HE WAS UNHOPPY.

What do you get when you swallow a caterpillar? BUTTERFLIES IN YOUR STOMACH!

How do birds grow strong? EGG-ERCISE.

FUN FACT!

Butterflies and tadpoles have exciting life cycles because they go through major changes in their features, called metamorphosis.

BRAINY BITS

How do brains say hello?
THE BRAIN WAVES.

What do you call an empty skull?
A NO-BRAINER.

What happens if you mix brains and bad weather?
A BRAINSTORM!

What did one brain say to the other?
"YOU SURE HAVE A LOT OF NERVE!"

FUN FACT!

Neuroscience is the study of the brain. Neuroscientists look at brain cells, called neurons, which make up nerves, which send messages between the brain and body.

GLOSSARY

biologist: A scientist who studies living things on Earth.

chemist: A scientist who studies what makes up the different substances on Earth and how they can change.

fault: A break in the crust of the earth.

gene: A tiny part of a cell that is passed along from one living thing to its offspring.

optimist: One who thinks positively.

physicist: A scientist who studies matter, energy, force, and motion, and the relationship among them.

sedimentary rock: The rock that forms when sand, stones, and other matter are pressed together over a long time.

solution: A mixture of substances.

tectonic plate: One of the moveable masses of rock that create Earth's surface.

trendsetter: One who sets a trend or makes something popular.

virus: A very tiny thing that can cause illness when it enters the body.

FOR MORE INFORMATION

BOOKS

McClure, Leigh. *Life Cycles*. Buffalo, NY: Cavendish Square Publishing, 2025.

Owen, Ruth. *Cells*. Minneapolis, MN: Bearport Publishing, 2024.

WEBSITES

Biology
kids.britannica.com/kids/article/biology/352855
Learn more about biology, the study of all living things!

Chemistry for Kids
www.ducksters.com/science/chemistry/
Learn fun facts about chemistry, from the different kinds of matter to the periodic table.

Publisher's note to educators and parents: Our editors have carefully reviewed these websites to ensure that they are suitable for students. Many websites change frequently, however, and we cannot guarantee that a site's future contents will continue to meet our high standards of quality and educational value. Be advised that students should be closely supervised whenever they access the internet.

INDEX

atoms, 10, 11
biologist, 4, 8
brains, 20, 21
cells, 4, 5, 8, 9, 21
chemistry, 6
DNA, 8, 9
experiments, 4
genes, 8, 9
gravity, 12, 13
life cycles, 19, 20

lightning, 16, 17
metamorphosis, 19
microscope, 4, 5
periodic table, 6, 7
physicist, 10, 11
rocks, 14, 15
space, 12, 13
tectonic plates, 14
virus, 4